Hezekiah's recovery. Or A sermon, shevving what use Hezekiah did, and all should make of their deliverance from sicknesse. First preached, and now published by Robert Harris, pastor of Hanwell (1630)

Robert Harris

Hezekiah's recovery. Or A sermon, shevving what use Hezekiah did, and all should make of their deliverance from sicknesse. First preached, and now published by Robert Harris, pastor of Hanwell

Harris, Robert, 1581-1658.

On Isaiah XXXVIII, 9-20.

Also issued as part of some copies of: Six sermons, preached on severall texts and occasions.

[8], 48 p.

London : Printed by Iohn Haviland for Iohn Bartlet, at the golden Cup in the Goldsmiths Row in Cheape-side, 1630.

STC (2nd ed.) / 12838

English

Early English Books Online (EEBO) Editions

Imagine holding history in your hands.

Now you can. Digitally preserved and previously accessible only through libraries as Early English Books Online, this rare material is now available in single print editions. Thousands of books written between 1475 and 1700 and ranging from religion to astronomy, medicine to music, can be delivered to your doorstep in individual volumes of high-quality historical reproductions.

We have been compiling these historic treasures for more than 70 years. Long before such a thing as "digital" even existed, ProQuest founder Eugene Power began the noble task of preserving the British Museum's collection on microfilm. He then sought out other rare and endangered titles, providing unparalleled access to these works and collaborating with the world's top academic institutions to make them widely available for the first time. This project furthers that original vision.

These texts have now made the full journey -- from their original printing-press versions available only in rare-book rooms to online library access to new single volumes made possible by the partnership between artifact preservation and modern printing technology. A portion of the proceeds from every book sold supports the libraries and institutions that made this collection possible, and that still work to preserve these invaluable treasures passed down through time.

This is history, traveling through time since the dawn of printing to your own personal library.

Initial Proquest EEBO Print Editions collections include:

Early Literature

This comprehensive collection begins with the famous Elizabethan Era that saw such literary giants as Chaucer, Shakespeare and Marlowe, as well as the introduction of the sonnet. Traveling through Jacobean and Restoration literature, the highlight of this series is the Pollard and Redgrave 1475-1640 selection of the rarest works from the English Renaissance.

Early Documents of World History

This collection combines early English perspectives on world history with documentation of Parliament records, royal decrees and military documents that reveal the delicate balance of Church and State in early English government. For social historians, almanacs and calendars offer insight into daily life of common citizens. This exhaustively complete series presents a thorough picture of history through the English Civil War.

Historical Almanacs

Historically, almanacs served a variety of purposes from the more practical, such as planting and harvesting crops and plotting nautical routes, to predicting the future through the movements of the stars. This collection provides a wide range of consecutive years of "almanacks" and calendars that depict a vast array of everyday life as it was several hundred years ago.

Early History of Astronomy & Space

Humankind has studied the skies for centuries, seeking to find our place in the universe. Some of the most important discoveries in the field of astronomy were made in these texts recorded by ancient stargazers, but almost as impactful were the perspectives of those who considered their discoveries to be heresy. Any independent astronomer will find this an invaluable collection of titles arguing the truth of the cosmic system.

Early History of Industry & Science

Acting as a kind of historical Wall Street, this collection of industry manuals and records explores the thriving industries of construction; textile, especially wool and linen; salt; livestock; and many more.

Early English Wit, Poetry & Satire

The power of literary device was never more in its prime than during this period of history, where a wide array of political and religious satire mocked the status quo and poetry called humankind to transcend the rigors of daily life through love, God or principle. This series comments on historical patterns of the human condition that are still visible today.

Early English Drama & Theatre

This collection needs no introduction, combining the works of some of the greatest canonical writers of all time, including many plays composed for royalty such as Queen Elizabeth I and King Edward VI. In addition, this series includes history and criticism of drama, as well as examinations of technique.

Early History of Travel & Geography

Offering a fascinating view into the perception of the world during the sixteenth and seventeenth centuries, this collection includes accounts of Columbus's discovery of the Americas and encompasses most of the Age of Discovery, during which Europeans and their descendants intensively explored and mapped the world. This series is a wealth of information from some the most groundbreaking explorers.

Early Fables & Fairy Tales

This series includes many translations, some illustrated, of some of the most well-known mythologies of today, including Aesop's Fables and English fairy tales, as well as many Greek, Latin and even Oriental parables and criticism and interpretation on the subject.

Early Documents of Language & Linguistics

The evolution of English and foreign languages is documented in these original texts studying and recording early philology from the study of a variety of languages including Greek, Latin and Chinese, as well as multilingual volumes, to current slang and obscure words. Translations from Latin, Hebrew and Aramaic, grammar treatises and even dictionaries and guides to translation make this collection rich in cultures from around the world.

Early History of the Law

With extensive collections of land tenure and business law "forms" in Great Britain, this is a comprehensive resource for all kinds of early English legal precedents from feudal to constitutional law, Jewish and Jesuit law, laws about public finance to food supply and forestry, and even "immoral conditions." An abundance of law dictionaries, philosophy and history and criticism completes this series.

Early History of Kings, Queens and Royalty

This collection includes debates on the divine right of kings, royal statutes and proclamations, and political ballads and songs as related to a number of English kings and queens, with notable concentrations on foreign rulers King Louis IX and King Louis XIV of France, and King Philip II of Spain. Writings on ancient rulers and royal tradition focus on Scottish and Roman kings, Cleopatra and the Biblical kings Nebuchadnezzar and Solomon.

Early History of Love, Marriage & Sex

Human relationships intrigued and baffled thinkers and writers well before the postmodern age of psychology and self-help. Now readers can access the insights and intricacies of Anglo-Saxon interactions in sex and love, marriage and politics, and the truth that lies somewhere in between action and thought.

Early History of Medicine, Health & Disease

This series includes fascinating studies on the human brain from as early as the 16th century, as well as early studies on the physiological effects of tobacco use. Anatomy texts, medical treatises and wound treatment are also discussed, revealing the exponential development of medical theory and practice over more than two hundred years.

Early History of Logic, Science and Math

The "hard sciences" developed exponentially during the 16th and 17th centuries, both relying upon centuries of tradition and adding to the foundation of modern application, as is evidenced by this extensive collection. This is a rich collection of practical mathematics as applied to business, carpentry and geography as well as explorations of mathematical instruments and arithmetic; logic and logicians such as Aristotle and Socrates; and a number of scientific disciplines from natural history to physics.

Early History of Military, War and Weaponry

Any professional or amateur student of war will thrill at the untold riches in this collection of war theory and practice in the early Western World. The Age of Discovery and Enlightenment was also a time of great political and religious unrest, revealed in accounts of conflicts such as the Wars of the Roses.

Early History of Food

This collection combines the commercial aspects of food handling, preservation and supply to the more specific aspects of canning and preserving, meat carving, brewing beer and even candy-making with fruits and flowers, with a large resource of cookery and recipe books. Not to be forgotten is a "the great eater of Kent," a study in food habits.

Early History of Religion

From the beginning of recorded history we have looked to the heavens for inspiration and guidance. In these early religious documents, sermons, and pamphlets, we see the spiritual impact on the lives of both royalty and the commoner. We also get insights into a clergy that was growing ever more powerful as a political force. This is one of the world's largest collections of religious works of this type, revealing much about our interpretation of the modern church and spirituality.

Early Social Customs

Social customs, human interaction and leisure are the driving force of any culture. These unique and quirky works give us a glimpse of interesting aspects of day-to-day life as it existed in an earlier time. With books on games, sports, traditions, festivals, and hobbies it is one of the most fascinating collections in the series.

biblio life
old books. new life.

The BiblioLife Network

This project was made possible in part by the BiblioLife Network (BLN), a project aimed at addressing some of the huge challenges facing book preservationists around the world. The BLN includes libraries, library networks, archives, subject matter experts, online communities and library service providers. We believe every book ever published should be available as a high-quality print reproduction; printed on-demand anywhere in the world. This insures the ongoing accessibility of the content and helps generate sustainable revenue for the libraries and organizations that work to preserve these important materials.

The following book is in the "public domain" and represents an authentic reproduction of the text as printed by the original publisher. While we have attempted to accurately maintain the integrity of the original work, there are sometimes problems with the original work or the micro-film from which the books were digitized. This can result in minor errors in reproduction. Possible imperfections include missing and blurred pages, poor pictures, markings and other reproduction issues beyond our control. Because this work is culturally important, we have made it available as part of our commitment to protecting, preserving, and promoting the world's literature.

GUIDE TO FOLD-OUTS MAPS and OVERSIZED IMAGES

The book you are reading was digitized from microfilm captured over the past thirty to forty years. Years after the creation of the original microfilm, the book was converted to digital files and made available in an online database.

In an online database, page images do not need to conform to the size restrictions found in a printed book. When converting these images back into a printed bound book, the page sizes are standardized in ways that maintain the detail of the original. For large images, such as fold-out maps, the original page image is split into two or more pages

Guidelines used to determine how to split the page image follows:

- Some images are split vertically; large images require vertical and horizontal splits.
- For horizontal splits, the content is split left to right.
- For vertical splits, the content is split from top to bottom.
- For both vertical and horizontal splits, the image is processed from top left to bottom right.

HEZEKIAH'S RECOVERY.

OR
A SERMON, SHEWING
what use HEZEKIAH did, and
all should make of their deliverance from sicknesse.

Firſt preached, and now publiſhed
by ROBERT HARRIS, Paſtor
of HANWELL.

LONDON,
Printed by *Iohn Haviland* for *Iohn Bartlet*, at the golden
Cup in the Goldſmiths Row in Cheape-ſide.
1 6 3 0.

TO THE PRESENT
READER, ESPECIALLY
to his once-Hearers about LONDON;
THE AUTHOR WISHETH
all peace and goodnesse.

MVch honoured, and respected in the Lord; its no time to dwel upon private passages, all our spare houres are too few for publike prayers and praises: of those I have said something already, I only adde this for the present. The estate of the Church abroad, our States assembled at home, challenge our utmost performances in that kinde. Of these I cannot (indeed, who can?) say enough. The mercies of God are wonderfull towards us, as men, as Christians, as English-Christians: When I lay our selves by other Nations and Churches, I cannot read what Moses said to his Israel, and not make it ours. Happy art thou O England, who is like unto thee, O people saved by the Lord? &c. Deut. 33.29. For what Nation is there so great, who hath God so nigh unto them (the onely glory of a Nation) as the Lord our God is, in all things that we call upon him for? Deut. 4.7. What publike suit did we ever preferre that did not prosper? instance one; nay judge, what could

Peters Enlargement.

A 2　　　　have

have beene done more for this Vineyard, than the Lord
hath not done in it? Esay. 4. If peace by way of bounty, we
have had it, if plenty, we have had it, if victory, we have
had it, if the Gospel, if all, we have had all, if we have lost
any thing, thanke unthankefulnesse, if we lose more, it will
bee our owne fault; for God takes no forfeiture, but what
unthankefulnesse makes. Let us not then stand still till the
Lord recover his owne from us, as once from Israel: but
whilest he blesses us, let us present him with his owne, and
shew our selves truly thankefull, whilest he is infinitely
bountifull. Now true thankfulnesse is not a lesson soone learned; 1. the thing it selfe is made up of many parcels: 2.
the party that undertakes it must be more than a man:
David, Psal. 9. 1. intimates so much, when for the matter,
he delivers it in foure parts: whereof, the first is acknow-
ledgment of God in all; the second, a cyphering and sum-
ming up of speciall mercies; the third, an expression of spirituall joy in God, as well as in his gifts; and the fourth, a
dedication of our songs and selves to his Name, Vers. 1, 2.
And for the manner, presses, 1. integrity, for subject and
object, Ver. 1, 2. sincerity, for affection and end, Vers. 2. If
then wee intend true thankefulnesse, we must so see Gods
Name written upon every token of his love, that withall,
we keepe a register of the chiefest, and so looke upon the
gift, that in it we relish the giver, and sacrifice our selves
to his Name. We be too short, if we arise no higher than to
Gods blessings: the blessed God is farre and farre beyond
all created blessings; he is better than health, than wealth,
than peace, than grace: all these be but streames that lead
us to the fountain, but beames that guide our eyes, to that
father of lights, to that Sonne of righteousnes, God reconci-
led, God incarnate; God, made ours by his owne gift and
goodnes, is our peace, our help, our health, our life, our every thing, as David can never say enough this way: & when
we see, and taste, and feele all comfort, sweetnes, happines in
him, and thereupon unite our selves to him, be transformed
into him, passe into him, as that holy Austen speakes, and

make

Hof.1.9.
1 Chr.29.14.

Pfal.9.

אָרַת unde ἀ"δω
& ᾠδη, Græcè.
For of ספר Cy-
phar seemes to
come.

Iam.1.17.

Mal 4.2.

Pf.18.1,2.

make him our joy, our feare, our trust, our Lord, our food, our house, our covering, our all, then, then are we truly thankefull. Let us not then looke upon health, peace, other blessings in themselves, looke upon them as they be in God; see him healing, blessing, saving : nay, looke not so much what he is to us, as what he is to the whole body: nay, what he is in his Christ, nay, what in his blessed selfe : how glorious, how rich, how good, how far above all creatures, all praises, all thoughts : O the preciousnes of his thoughts to us ! O the height, depth, breadth, length of his love in Nehemiah 9 5. *Christ ! these cannot be fadomed by a David, by a Paul : but O the boundlesse, bottomlesse sea of beauty, glory, excellency, power, wisdome, goodnesse, that is in the fountaine it selfe ! O the matchlesse splendor that is in that unapprochable light, that no mortall eye, no immortall Angell can behold ! here not to lose our selves in admiration, is not to love; not to be rapt and ravished with the Church, is not to praise aright : And thus we shall never praise, till we* Psal. 51. 15. *see the great God in the least mercy, and an universall good in particular blessings, nay, when we doe so, unlesse God open the mouth and inlarge the heart, our lips will not praise him : therefore we must have helpe from God, if ever we will sing to him : For as no man can define God* Aug. *without God, so neither can he praise him. Labour therefore to be fild with the fulnes of God, with the Word of God, Col. 3. 16. with the Spirit of God, Eph. 5. 13. with the comforts and goodnes of God, and then our mouths will be full of songs, then we shall sing to his Name; as the Prophet saith, magnifie him, live to him, doe all to him, which is true life,* Psal. 63. 5. *true thankefulnesse. This is that thankesgiving which here I call upon every Reader to perform, especially upon my selfe, and my Christian friends about the City. It hath pleased God to wound and heale us as he did Hezekiah, there are not many of us, who did not (I thinke) receive in our selves the sentence of death, as Hezekiah did: now we are restored to life againe, what should we doe, but sing with him all the dayes of our life ? I have begun to you, as I was then able,*

A 3.   *when*

The Epiſtle to the Reader.

when God, (after perſonall and domeſticall ſickneſſes) brought me into his Houſe; I beſeech you ſecond me, and let not any prejudice fruſtrate my exhortation.

Truth it is, I have not beene able to anſwer your loves, your deſires; but reckon that amongſt my croſſes, not my faults: Tis true, I undertook you with much feare, but that did flow from your ſufficiency, and mine owne inabilities. I left you quickly, tis true, and in ſo doing, if I did not deſerve praiſe, ſure I am I did pitty. Beloved, I never had, I never looke to have in this pilgrimage, that comfort in my labours that there I found: what daſhed ſo hopefull beginnings, time will ſpeake when I am ſpeechleſſe. In the meane, I am upon a better argument: When I ſpeak of man, I ſpeake of a poore nothing; I am now in ſpeech of the great King. Pſal. 45.1. When I ſpeak of mens infirmities, (as needs I muſt, if I will heal my ſelfe) I am raking in a channell; whileſt I am contemplating Gods excellencies, I am in a garden of ſpices: pardon me, if I preferre this to that; and in caſe I forget my owne name to magnifie Gods, and be content to receive a ſcar, that many may ſcape a wound, hold me excuſed: it ſuffices me that wiſdome is ſatisfied. As for wilfulnes (which will not yeeld to truth, beauſe it is wedded to fancy, and paſſion) and ignorance, (which names vertues and vices from the event) they are unſatisfiable. Me thinks this concluſion ſhould content modeſty. If at any time, in any thing I have given offence, I humbly crave a pardon, where none is given, none will be taken by the charitable: For the reſt, I ſay with that Angelical man, let them be honeſt, it ſufficeth, though I be as a reed, 2 Cor. 1. 17. as a reprobate, 2 Cor. 13. 7. And now my worthy friends, let me proceed in my exhortation, Should I not love you, I were not a man: for your love to me hath exceeded all deſert and expectation, and all the while ſome (by occaſion of your call) have gained more by my poore labours, than I can poſſibly loſe, I have no reaſon to repent me of this acquaintance, but more abundant cauſe of bleſſing God, and loving you, onely whereas I could not heretofore in perſon correſpond as was fit, let me at leaſt in

writing

Traducatur nomen ſervi ut appar. humanitas domini. Chry. ad Pop. Ant. hom. 11. Aug de Donatiſt. Felix ſcelus virtus vocatur, & contrà.

So Chryſ. of Paul.

writing make that expression of my love, that I am able, before I goe the way of all flesh. Now what expressions can be expected from a Preacher, but prayers, praises, exhortations, &c? When you dyed, I prayed for you as I could: now you live, I rejoyce with you, and call upon you to sing with me. And whereas (as tis well noted) we usually are best when worst, and live best when we dye fastest, I call upon you, as upon my selfe, to remember your selves, and not only cast (as the Heathen teaches) how to hold your owne, but rather to exceed.

I ever dealt freely with you, let me not now alter. Fame saith, that London is as covetous, as proud, as wanton, as secure as ever. I cannot beleeve it: it is almost impossible, that so great a judgement, so gracious a deliverance should so soone be buryed. Alas (London) thou hast as yet scarce buryed thy dead: the noise of bels, the cry of parents, the scrichings of thy widdowes are not yet out of thine eares, the grim face of death stands yet in thy sight, thy bloudy wounds are scarcely stanched as yet: If thou couldest forget judgements, thou canst not be unsensible of Gods mercyes and thy change. If London should, yet doe not you (Beloved,) let others security be your feare, others impenitency your sorrow; and the lesse others take to heart Gods great, Gods remarkeable works, by so much the more doe you improve the same to all holy purposes. More would I say to you, but that I have prevented my selfe in my more publike exhortation; both that and this (more privately spoken out of my speciall relation and affection to you) I now commend to your serious consideration and Gods blessing, who alone can speak to the heart, beseeching him who therefore threatens that he may not smite, to give us eyes to see plagues afarre off, and hearts to profit by lesse, that we may not feele plagues yet seven times more, yet seven times worse than all yet felt, Lev. 26.   Amen.

Hanwell, March 20.

Yours ever in the Lord,
ROB. HARRIS.

Optimos esse nos dum infirmi sumus. Plinius ep.l.7.Max. Tales esse sani perseveremus, &c. ibid.

Aug. in Iob. ep. Minatur poenas, ne poenas inferat. Theod. in Ezech. cap. 7.

HEZEKIAH'S
RECOVERY.

Esa. 38.9.

*The writing of Hezekiah King of Iudah, when he had
beene sicke, and was recovered of his sicknesse.*

OE here a double condition
and behaviour of King *Hezekiah*; 1. he was sicke, and
then he prayed : 2. he is recovered, and now he gives
thankes.

Our businesse lies in this
latter part, which is made
up of these two : 1. an Inscription, 2. a Description of the Song.

The Description presents unto us the parts of
it ; 1. an aggravation of *Hezekiah's* former misery ;
2. an amplification of the present mercy.

The Inscription acquaints us, 1. with the author of the Song, King *Hezekiah*. 2. with the nature of it, a Poem written. 3. with the argument
of it, a Song of thankesgiving for the removall of

B   sicknesse

ficknes, & reftoring of health. And firft to the firft:
the paffage is cleere, ficke *Hezekiah* prayes, &c.

Sicke *Hezekiah* prayes, found *Hezekiah* fings:
as comfort fucceeds his croffe, fo praifes his prayers. Hence this:

Doct. 1.

After prayers, praifes. Prayers and praifes doe
not fo enterfaire that they can never be fepara-
ted, neither is there any neceffitie of premifing
petitions to each particular thankfgiving; onely
in a generallitie this is regular, when we have removed afflictions by prayer, we fhould welcome
deliverances with fongs. So much was 1. eftabli-
fhed by Law, *Levit. 3. & 7.* after facrifices of pa-
cification, followed facrifices of payments and
thankfgiving. 2ly. ratified in the Gofpell. It is a
generall Canon, *Is any afflicted? what it? Let him
pray; Is any merry? what then? Let him fing.* Tis
not vnlawfull to pray in mirth, to fing in miferie,
ordinarily; but tis fimply neceffary in afflictions
to be prayerfull, in the midft of mercies to bee
thankfull, and to entertaine feverall conditions
with different behaviours. Hereof is it that the
Apoftle S. *Paul* doth fo often linke prayers and
thankfgivings together, as who would fay, when
the one is put over, you muft paffe to the other.
So much (3ly.) upon particular occafions is
1. prefcribed by God, 2. practifed by his Saints.
Particulars will not bee needfull to men, who
know the generall courfe of Scriptures. So much
(4ly.) S. *Iohn* foretels, and in a fort undertakes for
fucceeding ages, in his *Revelat.* What finging
there fhould be after perfecutions by Heathenifh
Rome,

Shelamim.

Rome, hee foretels in his fifth chap. what there was *Eusebius* reports; especially in his last booke: Againe, what songs should follow upon the Churches deliverance from Rome Christian, or other (whether seducers or persecutors) S. *John* fore-prophesies, time partly hath already, and more fully will hereafter discover. So much (5.) Education and Reason taught Heathens, and must perswade us. For, first, if wee looke to God, he is (as the prophet saith) worthy to bee praised; 1. all excellencie is his, therefore all honour, saith reason in Philosophers; 2. All Religion is due to Him, therefore all thankes, which is a religious act; for to the highest Majestie is due the lowest subjection, and that is Religion, which subjects the soule; 3. Hee is the first spring and author of good; all excellencie and honour is invested in him, and derived from him, and therfore must returne to him, *Rom.* 11.*ult.*

2 If we consider the thing it selfe; thankes is due after mercies received, and wee cannot withhold it without many incongruities: first (as is implied) Religion is violated, which tels us that we 1. owe to God all possible service; 2. that thanksgiving is a speciall worship, wherin we transferre all honour from creatures to God; *Psalm.* 50.*ult.* 3. that wee are no lesse bound to acknowledge Gods workings in our praises, than his willingnesse in our prayers.

2. Charitie is violated, which bids us love an enemy, much more a God; to blesse those that curse, much more those that blesse us; to over-

B 2   come

V. Iubilees of the reformed Churches.

Reas. 1.

Reas. 2.

v. Arist. Ethicks.

come evill with good, much more to answer goodnesse with goodnesse. Indeed kindnesse by the rules of friendship and love in the Heathens judgements, doth challenge either recompence, if we deale with our matches, or acknowledgement where the distance is great; and the greater this, the greater that. Now betwixt God and us the distance is infinite, and if twere possible our love and thankfulnes should fill up that distance, and extend it selfe into infinitenesse.

On the other side, not to bee as forward with our praises as prayers, argues base selfe-love and servility, and makes it appeare, that wee love not God but his gifts; nay, in truth that we secretly hate him. For we begrudge no man the praise of his kindnesse, but whom wee either envie or hate: now God is above the reach of our low envie; and therefore our lothnesse to acknowledge him, proceeds from our inbred enmity against him, when of the twaine we had rather deny his grace, than yeeld our selves beggers and dependants.

3. Iustice is violated: we owe God thankes, 1. in point of Law and covenant. Tis our profession, our promise, our cheesage and rent that is due to him: so that the Orator spake not over, when he intimated that Ingratitude was a kinde of Vnjustice. For what more unjust, than to detaine, against all desert and covenant, Gods right? 2. In point of morality and honesty; in manners we must reciprocate with men, much more with God: nor can hee be an honest man, who is not

Gratia specialis pars justitiæ. Cic. L. de invent.

ashamed

aſhamed to bee an unthankfull man.

3. If wee compare the duties, no reaſon but we ſhould bee as full of thanks as prayers : 1. I am ſure we have as many mercies as croſſes, comforts (in preſent and reverſion) as wants. 2. All our ſorrowes and afflictions are deſerved, all our comforts undeſerved : if that muſt not weaken our prayers, ſurely this muſt greaten our thanks. 3. Thankfulneſſe will become us as much as begging, nay (as the Prophet addes) as much benefit us, as much comfort us : Thankfulneſſe holds old mercies, and wins new; yea, greater thankfulneſſe is a ſurer evidence of love and ſincerity than prayer, and no leſſe a cauſe than a ſigne of joy ; if not ſenior to prayer in the world, yet of more laſting, at leaſt of more excellency in the world to come.

Reaſon 3

Chryſ ad pop.
Ant. hom. 11.

Once, it is at leaſt as needfull for us to give up praiſes as prayers, for theſe reaſons : Firſt, we are (for certaine) as forgetfull of the conſolations as of croſſes, nay more, becauſe we are more ſenſuall than intellectuall and fulleſt of ſelfe-love. Secondly, we are as likely to miſcarry in proſperity as in adverſity, unleſſe the one bee ſanctified by thankſgiving, as well as the other by prayer. As Croſſes without prayer will embitter us, ſo bleſſings without praiſes will ſwell us, and make us giddie, unleſſe wee allay our wine with ſome of this ſugar, thanks I meane, which is ſweet in it ſelfe, moſt comfortable to us, and more acceptable to God than ſweeteſt Wines or Incenſe.

Cant. 7. 9.

Well, we heare what ſhould be; now by way

Vſe 1.

B 3 of

of reflection lets doe two things: whereof the first is, see what we have done. Prayers and praises should succeed each other, as day doth night, summer winter, what say yr u? hath it bin so? the truth is, when I cast my thoughts backward unto publike proceedings, I find what doth somewhat comfort mee; I finde, first, that after publike humiliations in 88. our most happy Queene was most publike and solemne in her thankfgivings : next, after our deliverance in 1604. *Nov.* 5. a set time appointed for solemne praises; thirdly, after deliberation had, some thankfgivings added to our publike prayers. But when we looke into private passages, alas wee are all too blame : we goe to God in our distresses, as Turkes use to goe to their *Mahomet*, or others to their Lady, by troops and Caravans ; but when we be delivered, we returne like those Lepers in the Gospell, scarce one in ten, in twentie, in a hundred. To speake sooth, most of us have small reason to glorie in our prayers; they be too faint, too few, too much overrun with pride and unbeleefe: but in thankfgiving we are starke naught, worse than naught: first, wee will not see wood for trees, mercies for blessings ; when we cannot tell how to looke besides them, we will not fall upon them in our thoughts: wants wee see, and so are still craving; favours wee will not see, and so are never thankfull. When speech is of crosses, wee have all, crosses in body, crosses in soule, crosses in estate, crosses in friends, our life is made of crosses: when of mercies we can finde none about house,

no

no money in purse, no corne in barne; no comfort in the house, no friend in the world, wee see no land, nothing but sea.

Secondly, when wee see, wee will not speake: when we fall upon crosses, wee are eloquent beyond truth, we adde, we multiply, we arise in our discourse, like him in the Poet, I am twice, thrice miserable, nay ten times, nay twentie times, nay a thousand times miserable; But when it comes to mercies, we speake of them as malefactors doe of their faults, yeeld no more than what can be extorted from us, or proved against us, as if we were loth to peach God or our selves. Or if (thirdly) wee say any thing, it is rather to set up our selves than God, and the sacrifice is intended to our nets, wits, providence, more than to Gods mercy: in truth we serve our selves in praises as Ignorants doe in prayers, they set up flesh and establish merit, under a colour of prayer; and wee under a flourish and varnish (of God be thanked) vent our pride, and stroke our selves. The worst unthankfulnesse is, when men love not to be beholden to God. Or lastly, if something bee said, thats all, for little is done: True thankfulnesse stands in a reciprocation of affections & actions. We should returne love for love, and service at least for kindnesse; but wee doe not so. It fares with us as once with Israel; the eare, which tastes words as the taste doth meats, was so filled with choler, that they could relish no comfort (*Exod.* 6.9.) whilest *Moses* and *Aaron* spake: and our thoughts bee so sowred with the taste of crosses,

that.

Aristop. in Plut. Act.4 sc.3. κỳ τείσκακο-δαμων, κỳ τε-τράκις,κỳ πεν-τάκις, κỳ δωδů-κακις, κỳ μυεια-κις.

V. chrys. hom. 11. ad pop. Ant. Anim. tristi, non audit.

that we can taste no mercies, at least we cannot taste the sweetnesse of the giver in the gift ; and thence it is that our affections lie dead within us, whilst his mercies swarme about us. Hee shewes his power in the greatnesse, his wisdome in the seasonablenesse, his truth in the constancie, his grace in the freenesse, the riches of his mercies in the fulnesse of his blessings ; but nor one nor other affect us. Our hearts are so farre from *Davids* zeale hereupon, as that (like *Nabals*) they are either as cold or heavie as a stone. Miserable hearts, and miserably dead, when so many warming and reviving comforts cannot raise them upwards: but in the meane, what hope of quicke actions, when we labour with so dead affections ?

2 For deeds : true thankfulnesse improves the gift, to the givers honour. A friend gives me a Ring, Ile weare it for his sake ; a booke, Ile use it for his sake ; a Iewell, Ile keepe it for his sake, that is, so as may best expresse my love, and report his goodnesse. Were wee truly thankfull to our God, wee would use all his tokens for his sake; eat our meat to him, weare our clothes to him, spend our strength for him, live to him, sleepe to him, die for him : but (out upon our unthankfulnesse) we use his blessings as *Iehu* did *Iehorams* messengers; *David Goliah's* sword, we turne them against their Master, and fight against heaven with that health, wit, wealth, those friends, meanes, mercies that wee received thence. If this bee thankfulnes, to be so much the more proud, idle, secure, wanton, scornefull, impenitent, by how much

much the more we are enriched, advanced and blessed, I cannot tell who may be called unthankfull. Brethren, understand your selves, there is not this day a Nation under heaven more bound to God than we be; if now, we shal waste that time in spying out flawes in the State, and matter of complaint at home, that should be taken up in recounting mercies, 'tis just with God to lay us even with other distressed Churches, and to make us know what we had by what we want. If any place be yet left for admonition, be wee all advised to call to minde, with *Pharaoh's* Butler, this day our fault, even that fault which is our nationall sinne, the sinne of unthankfulnesse: and be it granted (by you and me, and by us all) that never people have had more cause, but taken lesse occasion of blessing God.

Gen. 41.9.

2 And now (to speake forward) let us take forth *Hezekiah's* lesson; after sighs let's send forth songs, as he did: nay, he in the midst of sorrowes can finde some matter of praise: nay, the Church when she only liv'd, could yet say, *It is his mercy that we have so much.* If the best people can sing in troubles, should not wee in peace? If they can when distressed, should not we when delivered? If they bee so sensible of one blessing, should not we of an hundred, of a thousand? It may be their undertakings in the day of affliction were more. No, in feares and sorrowes wee are as ready to vow and promise thanks as any; and if to promise, should we not to pay? It may be our deserts are greater. No, nor wee, nor they

Vfe 2.

2 Reg. 20. 19.

Lam. 3. 21.

of a that not are not consumed

Ob.

Anf.

Ob.

Sol.

C

can

can challenge any thing but by vertue of the promise, and that was theirs as much as ours: It may be their engagements were more than ours.

Ob.

No, whether we looke to the freenesse of the giver, or greatnesse of the gifts, we owe as much as who doth most.

Sol.

For the first, the Lord hath cast upon us blessings, not onely undeserved, but undesired, unexpected; he hath beene better to us than his promise, than our prayers, than our hopes: hee hath prevented us with some which wee never forethought, yea, done more for us than we are aware of; and he hath given us others which wee never durst once hope for. I thinke the man lives not, that ever durst promise to himselfe so many dayes of happinesse, so long a peace, so sudden a cure of the land, so flourishing a Church, so happie a time as wee have enjoyed; and what gifts more free than such as prevent all prayers, exceed all hopes, and are not only above but against all deserts?

For the second thing, which greatens a kindnesse, to wit, greatnesse and multitude of kindnesses, who is able to recount (particulars shall I say, nay) the severall kindes of them? First, we have blessings private, as many as soule & body, house and field, field and towne, towne and country can hold. Secondly, we have blessings publike and nationall beyond number: other nations bleed, we sleepe; others begge, wee abound; others starve, we surfet; others grope in the darke, our Sunne still shines; others are quite disjoynted and dismembred; they are members without

heads,

heads, heads without bodies, forlorne men, without Law, without Gospell, without Churches, or
Teachers, or Livings, or Bookes, or all: wee have
all; Magistrates, Ministers, Lawes, Trades,
Schooles, Churches, Townes, all, and all of the
best; of Kings the best, of Courts the best, of Law
the best, of Bookes the best, of Sermons the best,
of ayr, of fire, of water, of all the best: and can
we not yet set matter of thankfulnesse?

Ob. O but these be blessings saith one, they touch
not my particular.

Anf. No: doe have wee not all our private interests
in the publike weale? But speake in good ear-
nest, hast thou no particular favours? no blessings
privative, none positive? for shame yeeld both.

Ob. Yea, but where be they?

Anf. Nay where be they not? thou hast eyes, aske
the blinde whether that be not a blessing; thou
hast eares, aske the deafe whether that be not a
blessing; thou hast a tongue, what thinks the dumb
of that? thou hast hands, feet, wits, limbs, file,
bones, sinewes, veins, mercies enow betwixt head
& foot to fill a volume, is all this nothing? Nay tel
me, what way canst thou looke, but thou seest mercies? what canst thou touch, but thou feelest mercies? where canst thou tread, but thou standest on
mercies? But of what art thou compounded of
but of blessings? every sense, every joynt, every
sinue, every naile a blessing: nay, what is thy
house made of but blessings? what is it filled
with but blessings? blessings of the Barne, blessings of the Field, blessings of the Wombe, all
things:

blef.

V. Basil. in Iulit.
Mart.

blessings : nay, what's the World made of but
blessings? Heavens, Starres, Fire, Ayre, Water,
Earth, with all in the one, with all in the other
blessings ; all things blessings, all persons blessings, all estates blessings, all times blessings, as
S. *Paul* discourseth, 1 *Cor.* 3. *ult.* Now when the
Lord doth so lade us with benefits, and that daily, shall not we be thankfull? *Blesse,* saith our
Saviour, *when you are cursed* ; and shall wee not
blesse being thus blessed ?

All this while I speake nothing of spirituall
blessings ; indeed no tongue can reach them; we
can close them all within one word, one syllable;
God hath given us Christ ; but what a gift is that?
In him he hath given us a new world : the old

De iure.

world was forfeyted in a day, house, ground, fur-
niture, all forfeited in *Adam* ; then came in the
promised seed, the blessed seed Christ, and in him
all things are made new; new heavens, new earth,

2 Cor. 5. 17.

new Church, new tenure, all things renued, bet-
tered with infinite advantage to us, but cost to
Christ : What a thing was that, for the Creator
to become a creature, for life to dye, for happines
to weepe, for glory to be buffered, for immortalitie to bee buried ! O Lord Christ, who would
have done thus for an enemy, for a friend, besides
thy selfe ? But tis done; hee was made flesh, scene
of angels, slaine of men, laid in grave, raised to glorie, and we are now redeemed, justified, sanctified,
glorified in him. Redeemed, justified, sanctified,
glorified ! what words be these ? what things? No
man, no Angell can conceive the worth of these
things:

things : when we have said all, all is this, God
hath given us Christ, that is, God hath given us
himselfe, and all the creatures in heaven and earth.
God hath delivered us from the evill of all evils,
and hath given us the blessing of all blessings, the
marrow of all comforts ; the earth is ours, the
heavens ours, the word ours, the spirit ours, God
ours because Christ is ours. Now then when in
Christ our head wee are estated in the whole
world, have we not matter of thankfulnesse ? yes
(we now see it) if we had hearts.

But how shal's get a thankfull heart first, and
expresse it next ?   *Ob.*

Labour for three saving graces ; 1. Humilitie ;   *Anf.*
2. Faith; 3. Love. All these send a man abroad,
and make him seeke himselfe in others.

First, Humilitie empties a man of all great opi-
nions of the creature, and fills him with an high
admiration of the Creator. The humble man so
well understands himselfe, and other creatures,
and Gods excellencie, that he sees that too much
cannot be ascribed to God, too little to man: and
therefore he is very willing that God should carry
all the praise and glory from all creatures ; and
the more he can abase flesh and exalt God, the
more glad he is. Labour then to be humble men
with *Jacob,* and you will find your selves lesse than
the least favour, then you will see matter of thank-   V. Bradford
fulnesse there, where the proud finds matter of
murmuring.

Secondly, Faith is another emptying vertue: it
layes up all his treasure in anothers house, and

leaves it in anothers hands for feare of robbing. The faithfull mans treasure is Christ, his life is Christ, his crowne and glory is Christ: if Christ hath honour, he hath honour enough; therefore he willingly carries all to Christ. Labour then for faith: for if faith once unite you to Christ, that you be one, and unite you to God through Christ, that you can look upon God as your God, then you will seeke his honour as your owne.

Thirdly, love seekes not its owne (either profit or credit) it lives in another, and it works for another; in that measure that we love God, wee will seeke Gods glory, we will speake good of his name, and set out his praises. O love him who is love, beautie, nay glory, it selfe; and if thou love, thou praisest, as *Austen* speakes.

cinas & lau-
d.as. in Pf. 85. fc
& chryfad
pop. Aat. ho 6A.

Thus the heart will be tuned and set right, if it be a broken heart, a beleeving heart, a zealous heart, twill endite well, praises will streame from it as naturally as water from a fountaine, *Pfal. 45. 1.* but then (in the next place) the outward man must concurre, the tongue must walke apace like a swift pen; to that end, doe but owne thine owne words, first, take up the complaints thou madest in thine afflictions, be as eloquent in enlarging thy sorrowes now past, as thou wast then; speake now what paines, feares, griefes, finnes God hath now delivered thee from, as *Hezekiah* doth here: improve thy then forrowes to present thankfulnesse.

Secondly, recount thy vowes and promises then, call to minde what thoughts thou then hadst,

what

what vowes thou then mad'ſt; O if God would
this once helpe me, theſe faults ſhould be left,
and theſe duties done : now pay thy vowes.

1 Heare the other creatures, they ſing, &c.

2 Thy fleſh muſt rejoyce (as *David* ſpeakes)
in the Lord, thy face and countenance muſt take
up and looke cleerly, thy feet muſt be lift up as
Iacobs were, thy hands muſt be ſet on worke,
thankfulneſſe muſt be acted, not only talkt of.
Here know, firſt, that hee is moſt thankfull that
lives beſt, that leaves moſt faults and doth moſt
good.

Qui rectè agit Deum laudat. Aug. in Pſ. 34.

Secondly, that all we doe or forbeare, muſt be
done out of thankfulneſſe for what we already
hold, or have good bonds for.

Thirdly, that our thankes muſt in ſome mea-
ſure anſwer Gods mercy, and our former miſery;
the more our ſighs were, the more our ſongs
muſt be; the more prayers were made, the more
praiſes muſt follow, (for thoſe be double mercies that follow upon prayer.) And next for God;
the more remarkable the deliverance was; the
more ſolemne and hearty the thankſgiving muſt
be; for ſingular mercies we muſt doe ſome ſingular thing, ſet apart ſome time, ſome Preſent, ſome
gift, doe ſome thing that may ſeale up our hum-
bleſt acknowledgement of Gods goodneſſe, elſe
great mercies will worke great thoughts, as *Hezekiah* found for a time, 2 *Chron.* 32.25.

Now to particulars firſt; to the title, ſecondly,
to the body of the Song. The title acquaints us
with the qualitie of the Song, a Writing; the
matter.

matter of it, a Narration, 1. of his sicknesse; 2. of his recovery: which two parts make up the whole Song following.

For the first, the things inquirable about this Song are chiefly three: first, what kind of writing it is: secondly, by whom it was written: thirdly, for what use.

Which three questions shall receive these three short answers following.

1 The writing is Poeticall, and delivered in Verse, for the helpe both of memorie and affection.

2 For the Penman, we cannot say much of certaintie, nor is it much materiall; this is certaine, *Hezekiah* made either the descant or plain-song. 2. the Worthies of God, *Iob, David, Salomon*, &c. were much delighted with Poetry. 3. the Kings of Iudah (sundry of them) were endued with an extraordinary spirit, & a divine sentence was often in their mouthes, as wee see in the writings, and speeches, and prayers of divers of them: wherefore if wee say that *Hezekiah* pend this with his owne hand, we say no more than what seems reasonable in it selfe, & probable to others. Howbeit if any will contend (from the phrase) that the worke was *Esaias*, and the motion onely from *Hezekiah*, wee will not gainsay it: it sufficeth, that *Hezekiah* was the first mover; and that the Lord hath now pleased to adde it to the Canon, as he did also his Letters, 2. *Chron.* 30.

For the third question, the good Kings meaning was to consecrate (with this song) himselfe and

V. Sixt. Sen. & detensa in his *Hyg.*

V. Sanct. & Muscul. ad locum. *ergo* tis not so well entitled by the 70, ἐγ ϕδὴ

and his life to God, and to leave this upon record, as a pledge and proofe of his thankfulnesse to all posteritie.

In his practice, take notice of our duty.

Wee must adde to our present thankfgivings some pawne and monument of our thankfulnesse for the future. We must for great bleffings, stake downe present thanks: that's one duty, but that's not all; we must leave some monument thereof (we may) to posteritie, and cast how we may eternize Gods praises, and procure him honour in surviving ages.

This (first) God commands; *Tell it* (saith hee, when he speakes of great mercies) *to thy childrens children. i.e.* convey thankfulnesse to posteritie, and keep on foot Gods praises to the worlds end, if possible. Hereof is it, that the Lord sets a speciall Accent upon speciall mercies, and takes order that they may be reported to succession. Thus when he had set Israel over Iordan, and in possession of his countrey, *Set up* (saith hee) *stones,* some in the water, some on the land, that may witnesse my mercy, your thankfulnesse, for aftertimes; let the very place speake it. And elsewhere, Day unto day (as here place to place) must utter his goodnesse and mans gratitude. Hence those solemnities of the Passe-over for one mercy, of Pentecost for another, of Tabernacles for a third, of Trumpets for a fourth, of new Moones for a fifth, &c. God for great mercies would have a commemoration, a day of publike thankfgiving throughout all generations.

Doct. 1.

Iosh. 4. 7, 8, 9

Levit. 23.

D   Se-

Secondly, as God commanded, so his people practised this duty ; sometimes they set our time, as in the feast of Purim ; sometimes they set up altars, as *Abraham* often ; sometimes they leave a marke upon the place, as *Iehosaphat* in the valley of Beracah ; sometimes they multiply sacrifices, as *Salomon*, &c. sometimes they dedicate songs, as *David* often ; sometimes they present and hang up some monument of victory, recovery, or the like, as *David* Goliah's sword, *Gideon* his Ephod-like present, what ever it was, *Hezekiah* his Poeme, whether in parchment, brasse, marble, &c. and all this to this end, that Gods praises mought out-live them, and be sung by men as then unborne, as *David* speakes. Thus they of old, reason calls for the like from us.

1 T'is but civilitie to returne blessing for blessing : an Heathen will doe it. Now God blesses us beyond this life, not onely in heaven but upon earth, in our names, estates, posteritie, kindred; and why should not we future and prorogue our blessings beyond life also ?

2 T'is but honesty to pay our debts : now doe what we can, we shall dye in Gods debt. Sith we be not able to pay all at once, let's be paying in our heires and executors to the worlds end.

3 T'is a course we take with earthly benefactors, we would perpetuate their fame to eternitie if we could ; and doe we not owe more to God ?

4 T'is good policie to build Gods name, for then God wil build ours, as hee said to K. *David* of an house: if wee honour him, hee will honour us.

us. Indeed *Hezekiah* eternizeth his owne name in thus magnifying Gods.

1 Chr.32.32. 33.

Lastly, tis a sure evidence of our sinceritie and true love to Gods name, when wee desire that it may out-live ours, and be glorified by others as well as by our selves.

Having thus concluded the point, the application shall runne all one way, and this it is; VVhat so good a King practised, so great a God challengeth, so cleere reason perswadeth, let us now practise. Tell mee (my brethren) are not wee in Gods debt as well as *Hezekiah?* VVas not hee as thankfull for the present as we can bee? Are not we bound, to pay our debts, to edifie posteritie as much as he? VVell then, if you have as much cause as he, as great need as he, as many motives as hee, doe as he did, praise God with a lasting song; doe something that may set the world a singing when you are sleeping in the dust. Want ye as yet motives? Looke to your Father; his goodnesse lives for ever towards you, let your thanks be immortall to him: looke to your Redeemer; hee is the same for ever to you, be the same to him, in all manner of thankfulnesse: looke to predecessors; they have left us monuments of their love to God and us, lets reach them with advantage to posteritie: looke to successors; they heyre our sinnes and sorrowes, let's leave them some songs and matter of joy aswell as cause of mourning: looke to our Adversaries; they upbraid us, as *Penninnah* did *Hannah*, with our unfruitfulnesse: they crake that all our Churches, Hospitals, Col-

Vse.1.

Tis a signe of the best goodnesse to aime at publ. goods.

V. camp. alios &c.

leges

ledges are theirs. And albeit enough is said and
done already to breake the teeth of their slanders,
yet if possible lets (as our *S. Peter* adviseth) muzzle
them quite by doing more good.

You will say (perhaps) the lesson is good and
not unseasonable, but it concerns *Hezekiah,* great
men, rich men, learned men, that have meanes of
expressing themselves publikly ; but alas, wee
are poore, simple, obscure, &c.

Yea, but heare me; you are in Gods debt too, are
you not ? You must pay your debts, must you
not? Tenants must pay their rent, a cheesage, &c.
must they not ? well then, if you owe lesse, pay
lesse : if you hold not so much of your Land-lord
as another doth, yet I pray you pay for your cot-
tage, and for that you hold : you are a tenant to
God as well as King *Hezekiah,* pay your rent.

Ob. But twill not be accepted, tis so poore.

Sol. Come, that's a put-off ; a Marke by the
yeare from a Cottier, is accepted as welas an hundred pounds from a Farmer. Understand that
God weighs circumstances, and tis accepted ac-
cording to that a man hath : Goats haire pleases
him as well as Iewels from some hands ; two
mites as well as two millions. Hee needs not
gifts, he respects the giver, and tis possible for him
that hath but a subjects purse to have a kings
heart ; as tis said of *Araunah,* he was but a subject,
but yet gave like a King, 2 *Sam.* 24. 23.

Ob. O but we have no such encouragements to
give as *Hezekiah* had.

Sol. And why I pray ? God wrought a won-

wonderful deliverance for him; he hath wrought as great for thee, for mee, for us all, it may be bodily, certainly spirituall.

2. The world was not so bad then as now; a man can publish nothing but tis carpt at, settle no perpetuitie but tis perverted, Schools, Colleges, Hospitals, all abused. Come, come, this is but shifting: 1. the world is still like it selfe; all never were, never will be good: 2. these and such like objections were long since answered by *Salomon*, *Eccl. 1. 1.* view them at leasure. In the meane, marke what I say to thee: first, if thou canst not trust posteritie, and all honesty must needs die with thee, doe something whilst thou hast time, *Gal. 6.* O but, what's that to posteritie? Yes, Ile shew thee how thou mayest now lay a foundation for posteritie, and do that this yeare, this moneth, which may turne to Gods honour a thousand yeares hence. How is that? Thus: Art thou a father of children? 1. write Gods mercies upon their names (so thou be not phantasticall) and let thy children weare therein Gods praises to their graves; at least write them in their memories and hearts, tell thy children, and charge them to deliver it downwards to theirs, what God hath beene to thee, what great things he hath done in thy dayes, and so make walking Libraries and living Bookes of thy children: A godly posteritie is a breathing altar. 2. Are thou childlesse? yet set up an altar in thy house, worke thy people to heaven-ward, sow good seed amongst thy servants, and some of them and theirs may blesse God for thee an hun-

D 3 dred

dred yeares hence. Art thou a poore man? bee rich in grace, ready to every good worke, and thy name shall live when thou art dead: no men in Scripture more commended and renowned, than poore men and women; God himselfe writes their lives, and records their good deeds.

O but I am so poore, that I have no meanes of shewing my thankfulnesse. Doe not say so; hee never wanted meanes that did not want an heart; get that, and God will fit thee with opportunities as he hath with abilities. Never tell mee; thou mayst make the world the better for thee a great while hence, if thou wilt. How?

Videatur Rogers in Fox.

1 If thou wouldest borrow a little from backe and belly, twentie to one thou moughtest lend God something.

2 If that cannot be, say with *Peter, Act. 3. 6. Silver and gold I have none, but such as I have I give*; Ile pray, Ile worke, Ile advise, Ile plant, sow, doe something that shall doe good hereafter: there is not the least toe but it hath its use and excellency in the body. Art thou learned? doe good that way, as *Hezekiah* did. Some conceive him well

V. Tarnil.

seene in the Mathematicks (belike because of his buildings, water-courses, and the signe given him by God) howsoever, wee have his Epistle and Poeme extant, and they hold out instruction to the worlds end. If God hath given thee sufficiencie in this kinde, thou mayest speake thy minde to men yet unborne, and convey to them that light which God hath reached to thee. Be not too curious this way; thou seest that some in this

scrib.

scribling age set forth their owne wits, some their owne folly: doe thou set forth Gods praise, and ayme at mans good; write something (as thy gift is) that may doe posteritie good. We are infinitly bound to God for the blessing of Printing, and to our fathers for their labours: and wee of England are much to blame, if we leave not Arts and Tongues more refined and perfected than we found them, and the Scriptures more fully opened; no people living better furnished with meanes, no writings extant better accepted abroad, or to better purpose at home. O that in stead of triflers, Scholars would make themselves publike, and not burie their treasure with them like misers, or leave their works like fatherlesse children to the mercy of strange mid-wives, when themselves are gone.

V. Fox Mart. in H.6.

Art thou rich? let King *Hezekiah* be thy patterne: he was a good Common-wealths-man, he built much, he conveyed water to the Citie, hee fortified the land, and did good in warre and peace: 2. He was a good Church-man; he countenanced the Ministerie, he restored their meanes and livings, he repaired Gods house, advanced Gods worship, defaced the contrary. Thy place (haply) will not suffer thee to hold pace with him in all, yet follow him as thou maist: 1. as a citizen and member of the State, cast the publike good; see what good may be done in thy Ierusalem, the towne of thine aboad; see what houses need thy helpe, what grounds, what neighbours: here's a man over-rented, try whether thou canst not ease him;

Reade his life in Kings and Chron.

him; there's a man, wants corne for his land, stocke for his stuffe, helpe him; there's a third that hath will and skill to trade, but he wants credit; there's a fourth that could live with a little helpe, else he and his estate sinke. O come quickly before the man be drowned with all his family; a fifth there is that's able to breed some but not all his children, hence he is disheartned, take away one Lambe and put it to another Ewe.

2 When thou hast done so, cast thine eyes over *Iudah* with him; looke abroad, and see how present wants threaten posteritie with misery, and as thou canst prevent it:1. see how many grown ones there be that play, or steale, or beg for want of imployment, and set thy wits on worke to finde out some trade, some husbandry, some businesse that may give some imployment. 2. see how many little ones there be that mought be usefull if they had breeding; but alas their parents (if living) have neither meanes to breed them Scholars, nor money to binde them apprentices: call upon thy selfe and others, saying, There's a wittie childe, lets breed him a Scholar; there's a strong childe, lets traine him up for a Souldier, make him an apprentice, &c. who knowes what service hee may doe the Church or Country one day? O what good mought rich men doe this way, if they had hearts! If they feare to erect publike standing Schooles or Colleges, or to give some Fellowships for perpetuitie, let them (if they minde the common good) take some particular children that are most hopefull, and breed them,

in the Country, 2. in the Universitie till they be
fit for publike service. Here's no danger, unlesse
they will say, these may prove ill; which is with
the sluggard (*Pro. 26.13.*) to lye still, lest a Lion
should be in the street: doe thou goe on till thou
seest thy seed lost, and then stop there, and try another ground.

1. Bee, with *Hezekiah*, a good Churchman,
1. repaire Gods house, and let it never be said, that
our Churches lye like Barnes, and that *Our Father* lets downe what *Pater noster* set up. 2. Pro-
mote Gods worship, and allow some oyle to his
Lamps: doe not *Pharaoh-like* call for Bricke
without materials. What? expect Sermons, many Sermons; learning, much learning (so that
our Preacher must be able to answer any question) and yet deny him meanes! Meanes? by all
meanes we would have him have a competencie.
A competencie; how much is that? who shall
judge of that? Now the good Lord keepe his
Clergie from the vulgars competencie. I speake
what I know, and I speake it with a wet face and a
bleeding heart, I know Preachers of excellent
parts, that spend their strength in the Pulpit, who
cannot lay out fiftie shillings in five yeares upon
bookes, but they must fetch it either off the backs,
or out of the bellies of their poore children. Call
you this a competencie? Well, if we deserve no
kindnesse, yet doe us justice; lets have what your
fathers gave us. *Hezekiah* found things alienated
and turned out of course; no doubt wits were
working then: Take heed (Sir) of Innovations, of

E   making

making your Clergie too rich; the State hath thought fit to lessen their meanes: men can now prescribe against them, we can shew a composition, and prove our custome, &c. But what answers this good King? Custome me no custome, wee must not make a custome of robbing God. Were these things once Gods? either shew mee Gods release, or else restore them home. Now would I could say of him as a Father said of *Ahab*, *Hezekiah* ever lives, never dies: and the Lord put it into the heart of our noble *Hezekiah* to advise also about this point.

In the meane, let my speech to rich subjects proceed: Would you leave some proofe of your thankfu'nesse behinde you? follow those Worthies, who of late have gone before you in this kinde; hyre men to be honest in restoring to God his due: and if you have ought in your owne hands that of right belongs to the sonnes of the Prophets, heare God speaking to you in King *Abimelech*, Restore to the Prophet his owne, and he shall pray for you: if you doe not, his bloud in his children, the flesh upon his bodie, the anguish upon his spirit, the soules that depend upon him for food will cry against you, and will lay your houses levell with the ground. Do not turne off all with a Tush, Tythes were Leviticall, the Gospel speakes nothing of a Tenth, &c. 1. answer what's written; 2. shew us where the old apportion is reversed, and which is that *quota pars* now that conscience must rest in, and when that's done, then give us a just Commentary upon that, *Prov.* 20.25.

Amb. de Nab. quotidie nascatur Achab, &c.
In redeeming Church-livings.

Gen. 20.

V. Cartw. in Plut.

20.25.and tell us who hath authority to take that
(from a Church shall I say? nay) from God, that
hath beene once given him? And when you have
reduced and resolved all into a competencie, yet
let it be S. *Pauls* competencie, *Let him that preach-* 1.Cor.9
eth the Gospell live upon the Gospell, as hee that ma-
keth shooes, or heeles hose, lives upon his labour.
I speake no more than what every Scholar, who
is acquainted with a course of studie and reading,
knowes to be true: all that meanes which usually
is thought sufficient to defray all charges, to satis-
fie all payments, to answer all expectations of
wife and children for portions, of strangers for
hospitalitie, is little enough to buy a constant
Preacher bookes, and physicke. Now then, if you
will be competent arbitrators, allow him something more; some bread, some cloaths, something to keepe his wife and children from begging or starving.

You are wearie (I dare say) of this discourse, I
have now done, I have discharged my conscience
in delivering my errand, & have shewed you how
you may witnes your thankfulnesse to succeeding
times, if you please. There's first, your owne family and posteritie to bee moulded; secondly,
there be poore Orphans and children to be bred,
Schooles to be erected, poore Students in the U-
niversity to be maintained, poore Preachers to be
encouraged, Church Livings to be redeemed and
augmented: and if this be not sufficient, there be
poore Labourers to be imployed, poore debtors
to be releeved, young Tradesmen to be credited,

E 2   and

and if this doe not like you, there be in the countrey, fields to be trenched, woods to be planted,
high-wayes to be amended, correct-on-houses to
be builded, publike store-houses and Granaries
to be appointed, youths and souldiers to be tray-
ned; and in the Cities, waters to be conveyed,
fire-engins to bee invented, &c. And in both,
Churches to be repaired, prisons to be furnished
with some Teachers, and other imployments
more than a few: stand not idle now all the day
long, because none sets you on worke; House,
Towne, Field, Countrey, Citie, Church, Com-
mon-weale, Men, Women, Children, Tradesmen,
Church-men, blinde, lame, poore, all call upon
you to worke; nay, Christ saith, *Whilest it is day*
worke; the Spirit saith, *Whilest you have time, doe*
good; your Father saith, *Give to seaven and eight, be*
not weary in well-doing: your labour is not lost,
your cost is not lost, God will pay you all againe;
honour him he will honour you, blesse him hee
will blesse you, give him immortall praise, and
you shall receive an immortall Crowne.

We have heard, first, that King Hezekiah was
thankfull; secondly, that hee was thankfull to
purpose: Now lets see for what hee was so thankfull: 1. that his sicknesse was removed; 2. that
his health was restored. Wee will shut up both
in one.

Freedome from sicknesse, enjoying of health,
are two mercies which call for a due thankfulnesse. Need we prove this? First for sicknesse, we have
the voyce of God and man, that is banished, to

escape it ; 1. God promises freedome from it, as a
blessing upon the obedient ; 2. Hee threatens the
inflicting of it, as a judgement upon the rebelli-
ous, and accordingly proceeds.

Secondly, all men be of the same minde ; first,
good men wil blesse God for an Eagle-like body,
a body full of strength and life, *i.* of action and
motion like the Eagles, which is most lasting. *Pf.*
103. Secondly, naturall men ranke this in the
forefront of mercies ; yea, reckon of health as an
abridgement of all blessings, and of sicknesse as
the summe of all outward miseries. And that not
altogether without reason.

For first, sicknesse must be numbred amidst naturall evils : Howsoever it will stand with universall nature, and the all-wise God can improve it to
singular use, yet in it selfe, it must be deemed evill
in its nature, being against the private welfare of
the patient ; evill in its cause, mans sinne ; evill in
its terme and issue, it tends to death ; evill in its
effects, it adds to our miserie : whereas some evils
wound with sorrow, some threaten us with de-
struction, this doth both.

Secondly, it maimes nature, and hinders goodnesse ; the body is deprived of cheerefulnesse and
activitie, the soule disappointed ; like the Travel-
ler that rides a tyred horse, it can neither receive
that good, nor doe that good that otherwise it
could. There's no man knowes, but hee that knowes
sicknesse, what a disadvantage tis to the soule to
be lodged in a ruinous body. Its even stifled
within it selfe for want of motion, and move it
can-

Exod.15.26.
Lev.26.16.
Deut.28.22.

Thence called
ἀετὸς .S. Epi-
phan.

Malum contristi-
vum quod volunta-
ti, corruptivum
quod naturæ, con-
trariatus : est af-
flictus vitians acti-
onem. Galen.

cannot for want of organs, but very lamely : The
underſtanding is clouded, memorie weakned,
judgement dazled, phantaſie diſturbed, affections
diſtempered, in ſhort, the whole frame of Nature
ſo diſ-joynted, that like broken bones it can ney-
ther reſt nor move. Nor is the ſtroke onely upon
naturall actions, but upon morall alſo ; the ſoule
in diſeaſes chronicall becomes ſo lazie, liſtleſſe,
neutrall, that it hath no mind to pray, no ſtomack
to food, no heart to doe any thing for it ſelfe ; and
in diſeaſes more acute is ſo taken up and tranſpor-
ted with pain and anguiſh, that it minds nothing
but what cannot be had, ſleep and eaſe, &c. Hence
we may put that difference betweene ſicke and
ſound that the Heathen put betweene poore and
rich ; the healthfull man may ſtudie when hee
will, walke when he will, eat when hee will, ſleepe
when he will, worke, play, faſt, feaſt, ride, runne
when hee will ; but the ſickly man muſt ſtudie,
preach, travell, eat, ſleep when he can ; he is not
his owne to command : hee hath not himſelfe,
much leſſe other comforts. No marvell if ſick-
neſſe at one blow deprive us of the comfort of
our meats, beds, houſes, grounds, friends, wife,
children, &c. it deprives a man of himſelfe : hee
hath wit, but not the uſe of it ; memorie, but not
the benefit of it : yea, it turnes him well-moſt into
an Image ; he hath eyes, and ſcarcely ſees, eares,
and heares not ; mouth, and ſpeakes not ; feet, but
walkes not : nay yet further, thoſe ſenſes & parts
which let in comfort to the ſound, occaſion the
ſick mans trouble, the ſight of his cupps, glaſſes,
                                             boxes

boxes makes him ficke, the fmell of his meats
ficke, the tafte of his drinks ficke, the leaft noyfe
offends him, the leaft ayre pierces him, in a word,
this turnes his comforts into croffes, his bed tyres
him, his chaire troubles him, his friends difquiet
him ; their abfence offends him, and fo doth their
prefence ; their filence offends, and fo doth their
talke; their mirth doth, and fo doth their fadneffe:
poore man, fomewhat he would have, but he cannot tell what ; he is not well, and therefore nothing is well about him ; he is ficke, and fo all the
world is made of fickneffe to him, as to the giddie all things run round.

Now as fickneffe is a great affliction, fo health
as great a mercy : it comes from mercy, and pre-
fuppofes many bleffings; good temper, good
ayre, (at leaft for us) good food, at leaft a wonderfull bleffing upon poore meanes. 2. It tends to
mercy, health tends to life (the greateft bleffing)
to a long life, yea, immortalitie: fo farre as that
goes. 3. It carries with it a troope of mercies, 1. it
fweetens all other croffes and wants ; health ma-
keth thin coats warme, hard fare fweet, a meane
lodging good; tis the poore mans fawce at's ta-
ble, his cloke in his journey; his warming-pan in
his bed, his boots in the myre, and when he is at
worft he can leape and fay, as the countrey phrafe
is, Health is worth all. 2. It puts him into poffef-
fion of all other bleffings: 1. Hee enjoyes himfelfe, his wits, fenfes, limbs be his owne, hee hath
their ufe and fervice. 2. with himfelfe hee enjoyes
all things about him ; the light is pleafant, the

> Hence called
> in Hebr. length
> צרבה

ayre

ayre sweet, his meat good, drinke good, bed good, now all that was naught before becomes good. Againe, he relishes all, he findes contentment in all: now he sees a wife to be a wife, children to be children, friends to be friends, whereas before all the world was made of his humour, whether bitter or sowre. Not to be long; health is the just temper of nature; there all is quiet, cheerefull, fit for action: a good body helps the estate, the family, the soule; all within one, all upon him, all about him smile and prosper in time of health: and therefore this motion from sickenesse to health, *i.* from sadnesse to mirth, from paine to ease, from prison to libertie, from death to life, must needs be a happy motion, worthy thanks.

Actiores conservat & tuetur.
Backsinst.

Vse 1.

If sicknes needs many prayers, & health deserves many thanks; lets so bestow our selves, that if it be possible, wee may prevent the one, and enjoy the other: for the first, beware (to keepe mee to mine owne profession) of sinne, all sinne; sinne is the mother, sicknesse the daughter: man never saw the one, til he matcht himself with the other. More specially foure sorts of sinnes must bee as much abhor'd as sicknesse, as death.

Pro.5.9,11.

1 Sins of death: God hath adjudged whoredome, *Pro.* 5. murder, &c. and such like capital offences to sicknesse, to death.

2 Sam.3.29.

2 Sinnes of rebellion, committed against the cleere light and letter of the Word: these are threatned with all manner of diseases, *Levit.*16. *Deut.*28.

3 Sins

3 Sinnes of contemptuous prophanesse: the Lord hath said that he will be sanctified in all that come nigh him; And when any in their approaches were securely profane, the hand of God was upon their bodies, to death, or sicknesse: so *Nadab*,&c. so *Uzziah*, so 1.*Cor.*11.

4 Sinnes that have their root in the body, or at least worke powerfully upon the body. Of this sort wee name onely those three, which the Rabbins touch in one Proverb and three letters: The first is sinfull poverty, which at the first may seeme but little to impeach health; but if we look upon it in its cause, idlenesse, unthriftinesse, intemperance most an end; or in its effects, theft, robbery, &c. fretting; or in its companions, ill lodging, ill fare, ill clothing, &c. this may wel passe for one cause of weaknesse. The second is pride; a sinne that so swels the soule that it breaks the skin and case, the body: pride breaks the wits, witnesse *Nebuchadnezzar*; breakes the heart, and wounds it selfe, witnesse *Saul*, *Achitophel*, and breaks ones sleepe, ones peace, body, estate, all; a sick disease: a proud man is never without some ailement. The third is drunkennesse or intemperance: a man of this distemper, lies as open to diseases as an unwalled Towne to invasions and assaults. To him is woe, rednesse of face, &c. *Pro.*23. Brethren, if you would not be sicke, have nothing to doe with these fore-runners: prevent sicknesse in the cause.

For the second, Health; great *Salomon* hath written a Physicks for us, as well as Ethicks, in his

F   Pro-

Vid.Alsted.Rhet. Thus they conceited.

*Pro.*25.27,18.

Proverbs : there you may reade of the Countrey-
mans three Doctors, Quiet, Diet, Mirth. For the
first, health is nothing but Natures rest & repast;
health gives peace, and peace yeelds health : oute
ward peace is a great blessing, and very whole-
some, but that comes from peace within ; which
is double, 1. peace of Iustification; 2. peace of San-
&fication. So long, as there's warre in the conscience, warre in the affections, one power and
lust confl&ing with another, alas there's no more
quiet to us then was of old to *Rebecca*: but when
Faith heals the conscience, and Grace hushes the
affe&ions, & composes all within, then the soule
lookes out of the body, and sits in the face with a
cheerefull countenance. If your flesh, with *Davids*, shall rejoyce, labour for this peace; get faith
in Christs bloud, get the vertue of Christs resurrection, get wisdome, 1. all saving grace, and that
makes for health, and is a medicine; *Pro.3.8.*

2. For Dyet, *Salomon* gives rules, 1. for time,
*Eccl.*10.16.17.2. for qualitic, *Pro.*23. speaking of
wine-bibbers, fleshmongers, *Pro.*20.&3,&c. 3. for
quantitie ; eat not too much honey, which is
true in the letter : let not out thy appetite, lest it
cut thy throat, *Pro.*23,2. but rather be of the re-
straining hand, feed with feare, as *Iude* speakes,
rise with an appetite, and use the Emperours
Physicke, cure all exceedings by abstinence.

3. For mirth, *Salomon* is much in that argument: he 1. commends the thing, a good heart, i.a
cheerful heart is health to the bones, a very medicine: 2. he perswades the meanes, *Put sorrow from*
thy

Gen.26.

Pro.23.27.

V.M.Mason of
Fasting.

Aurelian

Pro.15.13.&
17.22.

thy heart (saith he) *reioyce with thy wife,* be lightsome in thy clothes, cheerefull at thy meales, &c. diligent in thy calling, than the which nothing is more availeable to comfort, after spirituall means of prayer, thanksgiving &c. And he that in Gods means puts himselfe into possession of these, shall arrive at so much health as shall be behoovefull.

Secondly, if this double blessing be worth double thankes, lets prize it accordingly, and praise God for it, and remember that there is a twofold deliverance; one which keeps us from sicknesse; another, that helps us out of sicknesse: a double blessing, one in continuing health without sicknesse, another in restoring health after sicknesse. If we enjoy either, let God have the praise, and conclude for thy body, as *Austen* for his soule, blesse God that hee hath kept off some, & taken off other sicknesses. For the first: there be some men who never knew what back-ach, tooth-ach, head-ach meant, they scarce know what tis to have a finger ake, at least they have enjoyed some good measure of health which hath its latitude; these men I confesse can hardly weigh sicknesse, or prize health: the best course will be to send them to an Hospitall, or to the house of mourning, there shall they finde silence, solitarinesse, sadnesse, light shut out, ayre shut out, misery shut in, children weeping, wife sighing; the husband groaning; Oh my head, O my backe, O my stomack, sicke, sick, sick, I cannot tell what to doe, where to rest, helpe me up, helpe me downe, O I sinke, I cannot stand, I cannot sit, I cannot lye, I

Vse 2.

Et que sici mala, & que non sci, &c. l. med.

Galen de san. tuend. l. 1. c. 4. 5.

F 2   can-

cannot eat, I cannot sleepe, I cannot live, I cannot die, O what shall I doe?

Brethren, if you have not felt sicknesse, yet heare it, view it, see how it racks and tortures a poore man, and that done, reflect upon thy selfe and say, O Lord, how much am I bound to thee for health! I can eat, my brother cannot; I can walke, he cannot; I sleepe all night, he never layes his eyes together; O Lord, give mee a mercifull heart to men, a thankfull heart to thee for this blessing.

For the second sort; have we beene sicke and now made sound? lay both estates together with *Hezekiah*, and provoke thy selfe to thankfulnesse. Call to minde what then thine anguish was, how sicke thy stomack was, how sad thy friends were, how tedious the night, how long the day, how terrible the thoughts of death, the apprehension of judgemen thinke now thy thoughts then, acknowledge now thy then purposes and vowes. Didst thou not then thinke, and promise, Oh, if God would reprive mee once more, I would become a new man, more carefull of my wayes, more thankfull for health than ever I have beene: thinke now what the price of health was then, what then thou wouldst have given for one nights sleep, one houres ease, one draught of drink, one vomit, one stoole, one the least of those mercies which now thou enjoyest? thinke how little wealth, house, land, friends, all seemed to thee without health, and now thou hast all restored againe in this, lift up thine eyes and hands to heaven with *Nebuchadnezzar*, and say, Sicknesse put me out of possession of all, but with health all is come backe againe; my stomack is come to mee, my sleepe, my flesh, my strength, my joy, my friends, my house, my wealth, all is returned: O what a change is here! earst nothing but pain, now nothing but ease; not long since stript of all, now possessed of all, as if I were another *Iob*.

Thus, would wee looke either downeward or backward, wee should become more thankfull; but in any case take that with you which is said before of thankfulnesse in generall, and apply it to this particular of health. Thankfulnesse stands not in words and complements: if you will bee truly thankfull for health, thus doe.

1. Come forth of affliction as *Iob* did, that is, as the gold comes out of the fire, purged from your drosse: let sicknesse draine the soule as well as bodie; and leave your humours, your pride, selfe-love, worldlinesse, hypocrisie, &c. weaker than it found them: and now you be made whole, take your Saviours *Item*, *Sinne no more, lest a worse thing happen to you*; fall not to your old dyet, lest you fall into your old diseases and re-lapse. The chiefest use of sicknesse is to be made after it: in sicknesse we must resolve against sin, our speciall sin; but after sicknesse we must second our resolutions with performances. Now then pay thy vowes, sinne over thy follies no more, but lay downe the practice of grosse sinnes, the pur-pose of all, & shun at least the occasions of them. And then in the second place, offer to God the

Nihil prodest verbis preferre virtutem, factis destruere vnitatem. Cypr. de mortal. Iob 23 10.

Ioh. 5. 14.

ran-

ranfome of thy life, as the Law runnes, *Exod.*31. I meane, leave fome feale and pawne of thy thankfulnesse to God, as *Hezekiah* did, nay as heathens did; they after a fhipwracke and danger, would offer fomething, after a fit of ficknesse would confecrate fomething to their gods. If thou wilt not be before-hand with Philiftims to offer in thy mifery, yet at leaft returne with the Samaritan, being recovered, and prefent fomething; let fome Church, fome Parifh, fome one Preacher, fome few poore men be witnesses of thy thankfulnesse, and bleffe God with and for thee. I fhall ever fufpect that thankfgiving, that fpends it felfe in empty words: the man truly thankfull, will make a fhift to pay his Phyfitian, much more to praife his God with hand as well as tongue. Reall thankfulnesse is the beft prefervative of health: let *Hezekiah* lengthen Gods praifes, and God will lengthen his dayes, and give him fuch a protection as never fubject had,

Nor is it fufficient to prefent the Lord once, and to confine our thankfulnesse to any one particular inftance; we muft, in the third place, confecrate our ftrengths and lives to God, and offer up our felves as living and acceptable facrifices to him, that is, wee muft ufe all our time, all our wit, all our health, every limbe, every thing that hee hath folded up in our health, to the fetting up of God in our hearts and lives; love him more than ever, feare him more, truft him more, pray more, reade more, heare more, do more worfhip, at leaft more purely than before in our Chriftian calling; and

V. d. C. de nat.: d or. l. 2 Tibul. clog. 1. ad Ifue. S. r. b. l. 8. Plut de oracul. Pyth.

Rom. 12.

Opus noftrum Pfalterium noftrum eft. Aug. in Pfal. 91.

and in our particular calling, be more upright,
constant, cheerefull, fruitfull than before; more
humble, more helpfull, more mercifull, more true,
just, charitable than before: in one, better Christians, better Church-men, better Common-
wealths men, better husbands, better Masters, better parents, children, servants than before. This,
this is true thankfulnesse, when we heale in soule
and body together, when we grow in spirituall
strength as well as in bodily, when wee spend all
that sufficiencie upon God and the publike,
which we have received from God; and this is
the thankfulnesse which I now call you and my
selfe unto, O be thus thankfull for your private
safetie, and for the publike. Our prayers for London, &c. have engaged us unto thankfulnesse for
them; for if we were bound to pray for them
being visited, wee are bound to praise God for
them being delivered: and would the one might
be as solemne as the other.

5 Now if we must be thankfull for others, must
we not for our selves? O my brethren, lets cast
an eye towards our head City, and see what deso-
lations are there made; goe into some places,
and there's silence: aske, where dwels such a one?
and the answer will be, hee is dead: where's his
wife? dead: where his children? dead: where
his man, his maid? dead: who is in the house?
death: and who dwels there? death; and who at
next house? death; and who next that? death;
death; pale death keeps shop, sits in the win-
dowes, seales up doores and holds possession,

This was
preached be-
fore the publike
thanksgiving.

50.

so that none dare enter. Passe from streets into
some houses, and what see you? some children,
but not father nor mother; aske, childe where's
father? gone; where's mother? gone, he knowes
not whither nor how. Passe on, and see in others
sad silent parents, mourning like *Rachel*, because
their children are not; To make the matter shorts,
doe but thinke what once their feares were, what
now their griefes are for their friends, then sicke,
now dead; and then come whom, and say, In
this common calamitie God hides our towne,
there's no crying in our streets, no tolling of
bells, no tumbling of carkases, no sealing up of
doores, brethren meet together in the Church,
neighbours together in the fields, parents dare
keepe their children by them, husbands and wives
live together; wee be not a terror or danger one
to another, but a comfort, a safeguard: O who
can be sufficiently thankfull for these mercies?
why should we whine for a few wants? we lacke
money, lacke corne, &c. O thou hast thy life for a
prey; thou, thy wife, thy children, thy man-ser-
vant, thy maid-servant, thy kindred, thy neighbours, thy cattell live, and life is more than ray-
ment, food, money, all things under Christ. Blesse
God for this, and say, I am poore, but yet I live;
my wife is sickly, but yet shee lives; my children
weake, lame, but yet they live: whilst there's life,
there's mercy; where there's mercy, there should
be thankfulnesse: the dead cannot, the living, the
living, saith *Hezekiah*, must praise God, and that
whilst living, as *David* speakes, *Pf.* 146.2.

POST-

POSTSCRIPT.

ANd here London, let me addresse one exhortation to thee: Hitherto we have stood amazed at thy misery and sudden change, sometime sorrow hath thrust out sad complaints, *How doth the Citie sit solitary that was full of people, &c. Lam.1.1.* sometimes silence hath swallowed up all words, and left us speechlesse, like *Iobs* friends: now me thought we heard thy inhabitants crying, *Is it nothing, &c. Lam.1.12.* now againe thy friends standing aloose for feare, as once men shall for Babel, crying out, *Alas, alas that great City, in one houre is thy judgement come, &c. Rev.18.* In this case thou wast not at leasure to heare, nor wee in case to speake: At such a time to tell thee of thy faults, had beene (as one who wanted no wit, spake) to upbraid thee with thy fortune, rather than to seeke thy reformation: But now the case is altered, the heavens are cleered, and thou with them. Now its time for all thy friends to call upon thee, for thee to call upon thy selfe. Wee have waited long to heare when thou wouldest say, O all ye that mourned for mee, now rejoyce with me, and repay as many thanks for me, as I have had prayers from you. Take heed, unthankfulnesse soone spends what prayers hath bin long in getting; forfeit not all againe for want of thanks. Looke upon *Hezekiah,* he was sicke and prayed, hee recovered and sung: If I should say that he was sicke of your sicknesse, I should not

Tacuimus quia tota civitas exhausta, &c. Chrys.hom.11. ad pop. Ant. Sir W. Ral.

G   say

V. Valef. fer.
Philof. Abulenf.
in 4. Reg.c.20.
q3.

say it without an Author: this I can say, his sicknes
was but personall, yet he is thankfull; what ever his
disease was, you will yeeld the plague to be a sicknesse, yea custome faith, The sicknes, The plague,
The visitation. This granted, there's great reason that thou shouldest be as thankfull for a thousand as hee for one, and adde deeds to words as
well as he: To this purpose, runne his method;
1. Make thy selfe sensible and mindfull of thy misery past: sicknesse is a rod, as the Gospell tells

ἀπὸ νόσων ἢ μα-
σίγων. Luc.7.
21.
Mic.6.9.

us; the voyce now to the City is, Heare the rod
& who appoints it. The rod hath a mouth, if thou
hast an eare; that speaks its errand, and gives thee
thy lesson. If thou wilt heare me, Ile deliver it to
thee with the same affection (degrees excepted)

Iob 34.31.

that *Elihu* did to *Iob, chap.*34.31.32.
Surely it is meet, and it becomes thee to say,
and that to God, I have borne chastisement; this
the first lesson. Farre be it from thee to say in thy
heart, Tis true, I have buried many children, but
what were they? of the baser & poorer sort, such,
whose lives were burdensome, whose deaths are
beneficiall to me: nor let it enter into thy heart
to thinke, Well, I see the error; had such a place
beene scoured, such traffike stayed, such meanes
used, this had beene prevented, hereafter Ile bee
wiser. No, it is thy wisdome to see Gods Name
written upon this rod, as *Micah* speakes, and to
acknowledge him: we wish thee to use all secon-
dary meanes, but not to rest there; thy experience
hath taught thee, that the plague nothing feares,
either thy new fields, or fresh waters, &c, it comes
of

of Gods errand, and when it comes, take know-
ledge of it, for it will not away without its errand.
Therefore in the second place, improve the affliction, as well as feele it; proceed to the second
lesson in *Iob,* and say, Ile sinne no more. First, see
why the rod is sent, as well as by who. The rod
buds not out of the dust, it hath a root, and that
root is sinne, and that sinne is manifold. A King
doth not use to smite downe his subjects by thousands for small offences; a father will not draw a
sword upon his children for toyes and trifles:
London, thou must take the height of thy sinnes
by the compasse of the punishment, and judge of
that by this.

What I have thought of thee, and thy government in generall, I have spoken elsewhere seaso-
nably enough, as I think; but now I speake to thee,
I earnestly intreat thee to take into thy consideration *Ezek.22.* and therein note how the Lord
charges her not onely with such crimes as were
committed by her, but also in her, *In thee,* saith
God, *were they,&c.*

For thine owne government and practice, I
cannot tell how to hope almost that it should be
much better in so populous and various a place,
nay, I know not the City under heaven, that's better ordred and disciplined: neverthelesse in such
a confluence of people of nations, it cannot be a-
voided but much sinne will be committed in thee,
if not by thee; and these sinnes, so farre as conni-
vence and basenesse makes thine, will endanger
thee. When therefore thou hast surveyed thine

owne

2.

Iob 5.6.

*Tuum est quod
tibi non displicet.
Hier.*

owne wayes, cast into the account thine other-
mens-sinnes, thine other-land-sinnes, thy Dutch
sinnes, thy French sinnes, thy Spanish sinnes, thy
Italian sinnes, thine-owne-countrey-sinnes; see
whether there be not in thee those that eat upon the mountaines, and chose that for lucre sake
both harbour and hide them. Whether in thee
there be not such as never yet saw Christs face,
or heard his voyce in the Assemblies: whether
in this wonderfull light, there be not in thee who
know not whether Christ be a man, or woman:
whether there be not in thee men, who study new
oaths and lyes, as men doe new fashions: whether in thee there be not who never see the Sab-
bath light, but lye either buried in bed, or drowned in drinke: whether in thee children be not so
wantonly bred, that they sleight father and mother; and, to make short of a long bed-roll, whether in thee there be not wretched men that set
open their doores to all the bankrupts, unthrifts,
gamesters, robbers, Cheaters, harlots that the
countrey pursues: whether in thee there be not
some that set all to sale, wife, childe, servant,
name, conscience, soule, all. And if upon search
these or any of these shall bee found within thy
walls or reach, O glorifie God in his visitation,
and save thy selfe by disclayming these sinnes.
Thine they be not, if thou where thou mayest
dost reforme them, and where thy power fayles
dost bewaile them. Howbeit this is not all; as
sinne must be seene, so must it be left: and therefore thou must proceed, and say, He offend no

more:

more: as a Christian, He reforme my selfe; as a
parent, my Children; as a Master, my family; as a
Magistrate, my charge; as a tradsman, my counsel.
And to the end thy reformation may be acceptable, learne two things more of *Elihu*, first, be willing to see and know thy faults, pray that God
would adde to correction instruction, that he will
open thine heart to heare, and some mouth to
speake home to thy case, thy soule; and when
light is comming winke not with thine eyes, shut
not the doore against it, Secondly, carry ever a-
bout thee this resolution, Let God teach, Ile
learne; speake, Ile heare; convince me of a sinne,
He leave it whatever becomes of me; be it my living, be it to me as my life, if God will say it is a
sinne, He leave it in the practise, in the purpose, in
the allowance of it; this murtherous sinne that
hath slaine my child, my friend, so many of my
neighbours, nay my Saviour, shall never have
place againe in my heart or house. And this is
not onely the way to thankfulnesse, but also a
proofe and peece of it: know that so many sinnes
as the love of God constraines us to leave, so many songs are presented to God; every slaine lust
is a gratulatory sacrifice.

Secondly, thou must proceed with *Hezekiah*,
and see from what, to what God hath brought
thee: shall a City conceive and bring forth in a
day? it hath beene so with thee. I may say of thy
sorrowes, what *Iob* speakes of his comforts, they
have beene swifter than a shuttle. Didst thou or
any man living thinke, that within one Summer

Verf. 31.

Psal. 94. 12.

Chryf. de Laude Dei.

Iob 7.

G 3   thou

thou shouldest burie so many, and so few weekely? could it be imagined, that when thy channels were discovered in so low an ebbe, that thy banks should be so suddenly filled againe? O London looke upon thy selfe, and wonder at thy selfe: invert now *Ieremies* lamentation, and say, How is the solitary Citie become full! how is shee that was barren, made fruitfull! Sit downe with *Hezekiah*, and consider what thy bitternesse was when death walkt in the streets, raged in the chambers, when death was in the pot, in the bed, in the dish, in the hall, in the parlour, when the bells spake nothing but death, the doors presented nothing but death, and every man thou sawest, thing thou touchest, place thou satest in, threatned thee with death: consider what thy cares, feares, griefs, thoughts were then; and now whilest thine eyes behold as it were a resurrection to life, so that now life is in the streets, life in the house, life in the Church, trading, building, singing, &c. alive againe, blesse thy G.o.d that hath wrought this change, and get up with *Hezekiah* to the house of the Lord: Strange it was, that hee in so short a space should measure the whole distance betwixt death and life; yesterday dead in nature, as unlikely to live as the sunne to goe backward, and to morrow so strong that he could shew himselfe in the Lords courts: This is wonderfull, and this made him wondrous thankfull. And what (I pray) wants thy deliverance of this? how much lesse wonderfull? how fast did sicknesse come in, how fast did it gallop out? how fast did it rise from

scores

See the plague at Alex. in Cypr. & Eus.

scores to thousands; how fast did to fall againe
from thousands to scores: O London; lay those
things together, and forget not him who hath
done so great things for thee.

In the third place, *Hezekiah* loves not to dis-
patch all at one journey: He begins his song as
soone as mought be, but it is not ended yet; he hath
left a patterne for thee to worke by. Thinke it not
sufficient to complement God with a few words,
and a short song, for a long deliverance; write
this mercy with a pen of Diamond, in a booke of
Marble; call upon all within thee, as *David* did   Psal.103.1.
within him, to speake of this deliverance to childrens children; and doe something that may set
men on singing 500. yeares hence: Thou hast
sonnes of all sorts; some Enginers, some Artists,
some Poets, some of excellent invention, some
of great activity, some very daring and under-
taking, some strong, some wise, some rich, of all
ranks some; call upon them, some to write, some
to build, some to invent, some to give, that Citie,
Country, Church, State, sea and land may take occasion thence of blessing God, whilst London or
England stands. Now happy *Hezekiah*, and happy, sicknesse of his that ended so well: his afflictions sent him to God with prayers, his recovery
with praises; nor God, nor man lost by this bar-
gaine: God had more service, *Hezekiah* more experience, we gaine a good copy, and *Hezekiah*
hath his lease renewed for fifteene yeares: And
thus afflictions conclude, which begin with prayer and end in thankfulnesse. London, make thy
selfe

selfe againe by thy ... ... thy ... met prayers, grow more wife, holy, humble, temperate, just, mercifull, fruitfull, and thou art a winner; thy gaines exceed thy losses present, and for the future, thou hast opened a faire prospect to a constant peace. The best security from future miseries, is to profit by former: beleeve it, thou canst not rake a better medicine against the Plague, than to profit by what is past. Now the Lord hath promised to teach us to profit, by *Esay*, and he performe it for his mercies fake, that so the controversie may end here, and the Lord may not bee put to saddle his pale horse of famine, which hath made parents to eat up their children once, and to wish them alive againe, that they might eat them againe. *Amen.*

FINIS.

LaVergne, TN USA
11 August 2010
193033LV00003B/25/P

9 781171 321569